GROWING UP

AGAINST THE ODDS

Created and Produced by Firecrest Books Ltd
in association with John Francis/Bernard Thornton Artists

Copyright © 2000 Firecrest Books Ltd
and Copyright © 2000 John Francis/Bernard Thornton Artists

Published by Tangerine Press™, an imprint of Scholastic Inc.
555 Broadway, New York, NY 10012

Tangerine Press™ and associated logo and design are trademarks of Scholastic Inc.

ISBN 0-439-24960-0

Printed and bound in Belgium
First printing December 2000

GROWING UP

AGAINST THE ODDS

Bernard Stonehouse

Illustrated by
John Francis

TANGERINE PRESS™ and associated logo
and design are trademarks of Scholastic Inc.

FOR MALCOLM

Art and Editorial Direction by
Peter Sackett

Designed by
Paul Richards, Designers & Partners

Edited by
Norman Barrett

Color separation by
Sang Choy International Pte. Ltd.
Singapore

Printed and bound by
Casterman, Belgium

CONTENTS

Introduction

Growing up in the animal world is a risky business. Although grown-up animals are always well adapted to deal with their environment, young ones are less fortunate and more often at risk. Smaller and weaker than their parents, they are more liable to be caught unaware by such natural dangers as rain, strong winds, and snow.

And they are less able to defend themselves against predators. In their shorter lives, young animals have had fewer chances to learn how dangerous the world can be. It is not surprising that, though millions of young animals come into the world each year, all but a very few die within the first few weeks of life. Those that survive have made it – against the odds.

Here a young blue tit, a close relative of the American chickadee, is learning about life the hard way. Just one month out of the egg, and two weeks out of the nest, it has caught the attention of a domestic cat, and the cat wants it for supper. One of a family of ten that left the nest, it may already be the only survivor – especially if the cat has been busy before. If it gets away, it might remember that furry animals with whiskers, pointed ears, and a long tail mean danger, and keep out of their reach.

Wandering albatross

This young wandering albatross, ten months old and wearing the last of its down, is being fed by one of its parents. It has waited ten days for its meal. Returning this morning with a full crop, the parent landed close to the nest, greeting its chick with noisy cackles. Then, in answer to the chick's calls, it vomited up fish and squid, which the chick took, piece by messy piece, from its bill. Now there is no more left. By this evening, the parent will have flown off to search the seas for more.

In another ten days or so, the other parent will bring a similar meal. It is winter, the sea is rough, and food is hard to find. Between meals, the young bird sits alone on the nest, through snowstorms and icy rain, watching the windy sky. From time to time, it stretches its muscles and exercises its floppy wings. In another couple of months, it will be ready to fly. Meanwhile, it depends entirely on its parents, and those occasional, very welcome warm breakfasts.

When almost fully grown, chicks strengthen their flight muscles by spreading and flapping their wings.

At 12 months, the young albatross is ready to fly off on its own. Largest of all seabirds, wandering albatrosses reach a weight of 30 lbs. (13 kg), with wings spanning more than 11 ft. (3.3 m). They live only in the southern hemisphere, nesting on the windward slopes of cold, remote islands.

Zebra

Here is a zebra foal, born just a few minutes ago, trying to stand for the first time. The foal is finding its long legs hard to manage. Its mother, standing behind, gives it a helping nudge. Other members of the herd stand around, forming a barrier between the foal and any lions, hyenas, or other predators that may want to attack.

Zebras are closely related to horses, and very much like them in shape and size. The most obvious differences are the broad or narrow black stripes covering their head, body, and legs. They live on the plains of eastern and southern Africa, in herds of a dozen or more. The herds move constantly. Within an hour or so, this baby will be trotting, still rather unsteadily, alongside its mother, with six or seven other mares (females) and a stallion (male) close by.

Like horses, zebras feed mainly on grass. The foal will feed for several days on its mother's milk. But after a week or so, it will put its head down like the older members of the herd, and start to graze. If the foal survives all the dangers, in three or four years' time it may well have a foal of its own.

Less than an hour after birth, the foal finds her mother's milk.

Zebras often travel with herds of antelopes, gnus, or other animals. This helps to keep them and their young safe from predators.

Leopard

Leopards are members of the cat family that hunt on the African plains. You seldom see more than one adult at a time. Two or more leopards together are likely to be a mother with half-grown cubs. As with most other cats, males play no part in rearing the young. Female leopards produce their cubs, usually a litter of three or four, and raise them on their own.

This mother leopard has a family of four. About five weeks old, the cubs are big enough to walk and take an interest in their surroundings. But the plains are full of danger. The cubs lie low in a den, which is just a small hollow among the rocks, while their mother goes out hunting. They sleep most of the day and wake up in the evening. They tumble and play together like kittens until their mother returns. If they are lucky, she will bring meat, perhaps an antelope or small reptile that she has caught and killed.

While she is away, the cubs are in constant danger from predators. These could be hunting dogs, jackals, or hyenas attracted by their scent, or sharp-eyed hawks that have spotted where they live from the air. To give her cubs a better chance of surviving, every two or three days the mother leopard picks them up in her mouth, one by one, and carries them gently to another lair.

Later, they will learn to hunt with her, and in a few months will be independent. Only one or two of the four will live long enough to have cubs of their own.

Leopard cubs in their first weeks have much to learn. This one is trying to stalk and catch a meal ...

... and this one is finding out about tree climbing.

12

Prairie dog

rairie dogs live on the prairies, or grasslands, of North America. Despite their name, they are not dogs. They are squirrellike rodents with short tails. They live in burrows and feed in groups on grass and other soft vegetation. Why call them dogs? Because, when alarmed by the sight of a predatory coyote or hawk, they bark a warning like terriers.

As they feed among the short grass, dozens of pairs of eyes scan the sky for predators. This mother has spotted a prairie hawk and has started to bark – a general warning that sends the whole group scurrying below.

They live in huge colonies called towns, often numbering in the thousands of burrows. Each town is divided into wards, and each ward is subdivided into smaller groups of burrows, with several entrances leading to a network of underground tunnels. These are home to a family of three or four females and a half dozen males, usually bossed by a single older male. The tunnel entrances are ringed by walls of earth up to 18 inches (45 cm) high, to keep out floodwater when it rains.

Female prairie dogs produce litters of three or four young in nests within the tunnels. When several give birth around the same time, the young are brought up together. Though hostile to neighbors, members of the family feed together, recognizing each other by scent and exchange of "kisses," which bring them into close body contact. Keeping together, and warning one another of danger, increases their chances of survival in a dangerous world.

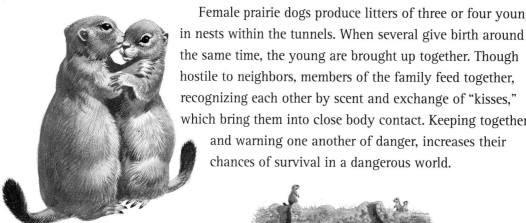

These prairie dogs, an adult and near-adult young, are "kissing" – coming close so they can recognize each other by sight and scent.

Entrances at the surface link a complex of tunnels and chambers in which families of prairie dogs live, sleep, and bear their young.

Gorilla

How does a young gorilla learn which plants are good to eat and which are too tough or poisonous? A gorilla troop or family usually has one big male (called a silverback because of the silvery-gray fur on his back), leading two or more females with their babies. While it is small, the baby is carried along clinging to its mother. When tiny, it hangs on in front, where it can easily reach her milk.

As the baby gets bigger, it spends more time on her back. This is more comfortable for both of them. From there, as she moves through the forest, the youngster can see and think about the world ahead. With the troop around it, the baby is relatively safe from predators.

Here is an infant, nearly six months old, watching over its mother's shoulder. It watches the other gorillas in the group, and how they behave toward one another. It watches sunlight and shadows, birds and butterflies. Perhaps most important of all, it watches its mother feeding, noticing in particular which leaves and shoot she chooses.

From time to time, the youngster reaches over to try some. It grasps a branch, sniffs it carefully, takes a bite, chews it, and tastes the juices. Some that may be too tough or too bitter are spat out. Some taste very good, and the baby gorilla begins to look out for more. Although its mother is still feeding it on milk, the baby's interest in more solid foods grows every day. This is how it safely learns how to add different foods to its diet.

A first adventure – while the troop rests, the young gorilla leaves its mother to scramble among the lower tree branches.

From its mother's back, the youngster gets to know its family – the other members of the troop, who help to protect it from danger.

Bald eagle

Majestic black-and-white birds, with wings spanning more than 6 feet 6 inches (2 m), bald eagles were once common all over the United States. They are the U.S. national bird. Hunting and chemical poisons destroyed them at many of their former breeding grounds. But they survived, mainly in wilderness areas of Alaska and Florida, and are now becoming less rare in other places. They are not really bald. The white feathers on the head and neck, contrasting with the dark body feathers, make them look bald from a distance.

Bald eagles nest in tall trees or on rocky cliffs. Year after year in spring, pairs return to the same nest sites, piling up more sticks and branches to create huge, untidy, and very smelly nests. Females lay two white or pale blue eggs, which the partners take turns to incubate for five weeks. Then they share the duties of brooding and feeding the chicks.

At first, only one parent goes off at a time, leaving the other on guard. As the chicks grow bigger, they need more food than one parent alone can bring. When the chicks are big enough to defend themselves against gulls and other small predators, both parents can hunt at the same time. This male eagle has brought a salmon back to the nest, and is tearing it with its bill and claws to feed pieces to the two hungry nestlings. Soon, the female will fly in with a similar offering. It takes dozens of fish to feed two growing eaglets. If one of the parents dies, the chicks are likely to die, too.

This young eagle, still in dark plumage, has swooped down and plucked a salmon – its first catch – from the surface of the sea.

Chicks are fully fledged and ready to fly about 12 weeks after hatching.

King penguin

We are on South Georgia, an island in the cold Southern Ocean, among a breeding colony of king penguins. The sleek one with orange throat patches is an adult. The woolly-looking ones in thick brown down are chicks. There are about 5,000 chicks in the colony. It is late May, the end of summer. Some of the chicks were hatched in January or February, and are already quite big. The smaller ones are only one to two months old.

The chicks are too young to swim. Their parents bring fish and squid in their crops from the sea. They will have to feed them like this all through the winter, because kings are big penguins and the chicks take almost a year to grow. Winters are bitterly cold, with strong winds, and there is not much food in the sea. The chicks will huddle together to keep warm. They will be fed only once every two or three weeks. Many of the smaller ones, like the two smallest shown here, will almost certainly die of starvation before spring.

King penguins make no nests. They carry the single egg, and later the small chick, on their feet.

Kings feed their chicks by regurgitating (vomiting) food from the crop into the back of the throat, which is where the chick takes it from.

Weddell seal

It is a cold, clear September morning in Antarctica, and this Weddell seal pup is having its first swim. It is early spring, so still very cold. The temperature is about -4°F (–20°C) and the sea is frozen over. The pup was born on the sea ice about three weeks ago. It was quite a shock. It had been living and growing in a warm cavity inside its mother for eight or nine months, and then was suddenly in a frozen world. This pup is one of the lucky ones. Very cold weather is a killer of newborn pups. Mother has been sheltering her baby with her body from the coldest winds, and feeding it on rich milk. This has given the baby a layer of fat under its skin that helps it keep warm.

Seals are warm-blooded mammals, distantly related to bears. Their arms and legs are flat and paddlelike, making it hard for them to move on land, but helping them to swim superbly. They feed on fish, squid, and shrimp, which are generally more plentiful in cold seas than in warm. So most seals live in the colder oceans. This kind lives in the coldest parts of the Southern Ocean surrounding Antarctica. The pup followed its mother through a hole in the sea ice. Swimming came naturally to the pup, but it has had enough, and is figuring out how to get back onto the ice. When the pup makes it, there'll be a supper of warm, creamy milk.

A Weddell seal pup grows quickly on its mother's milk. About 65 lbs. (30 kg) at birth, it weighs twice as much in ten days ...

... and three times as much in five to six weeks, when it starts to feed for itself.

Pintailed sandgrouse

It is hot, very hot, in the central Asian desert. There are no trees or shrubs to provide shade. This pintailed sandgrouse is nesting in the open. It is called a "pintail" because its tail feathers come to a sharp point. In the early morning, the sitting bird gets shade and shelter from the rocks nearby, but at midday it is under the full glare of the sun. The nest is a simple hollow in the sand. The three eggs, and the chicks that hatch from them, are colored to match the background. They need to be, for they are sitting targets for sharp-eyed predators in the skies above them.

Now it is evening. The hen sat all day on the nest, but the cock has now relieved her, and he will keep watch all night. The hen was very thirsty, and has flown off to a pool several miles away to find water. The cock has just arrived from the pool, where the last thing he did was soak the feathers of his chest and belly. The feathers are still dripping wet, and the chicks, just a few days old, are running their bills through them to take their first drink. Then they will settle for the night, in cool, damp darkness under his wings.

In their sandy nest, the round, speckled eggs of the sandgrouse look something like pebbles ...

... and so do the chicks, making it difficult for hawks and other predators to spot them.

Leatherback turtle

Adult leatherback turtles live in warm tropical seas and are huge, weighing as much as 1,800 pounds (800 kg). They swim well, and feed on jellyfish and other slow-moving, soft-bodied animals of the sea surface. Adult males spend all of their lives in water. Adult females come ashore only for a few hours two or three times a year, to lay their eggs.

One night seven weeks ago, a female leatherback crawled ashore on this tropical beach. She dug a deep pit in the sand above the high-tide mark, using her flippers as shovels. At the bottom, she laid 60 to 80 soft-shelled white eggs, much like oversized Ping Pong balls. Then she scooped the sand back to cover them and returned to the sea. Now 60 or more tiny, matchbox-sized turtles have hatched and popped up through the sand, and are lining themselves up for a rush down to the sea. The black vulture is wondering which one to eat first. The bird will grab five or six. The rest will get away. But the sea, too, is a dangerous place for tiny turtles, with many predatory fish. Very few will survive even their first month.

Left entirely to themselves, the eggs take about seven weeks to hatch, and the young turtles scramble up through the warm sand.

The adult turtle is almost 6 ft. (2 m) long, the newly hatched babies are only 2 in. (5 cm).

Black spider monkey

Sixty-five feet (20 m) or more above the ground, in a South American jungle, a mother spider monkey is swinging through the treetops, using both hands, both feet, and her tail. Clinging tightly to her chest is her month-old infant. It seems a dangerous way to bring up baby.

The mother is in a hurry. Together with a dozen others, she has been feeding high in the trees on fruit and leaves. From time to time she has fed her baby from the milk glands on her chest. Now something has scared her, perhaps a snake or a predatory bird. With the rest of her group, she is swinging her way down to a safer place.

All day and every day, this is how she lives. Why does she take the baby with her? Because the forest is full of dangers for baby monkeys, too. Leaving it behind in a nest or on a branch would be even more risky than carrying it with her.

The baby just hangs on. Before long, if it survives, it, too, will be a treetop swinger, in search of its own fruit and leaves.

The young spider monkey quickly learns how to hang from a branch by the tail, using its hands to pick fruit.

Manatee

Manatees look a bit like seals, but are quite unrelated, and live much quieter lives. Seals are hunters that chase after fish, squid, and shrimp. Manatees are herbivores, eating only vegetation. Sailors called them sea cows – a good name for animals that live in herds and graze on grass. They swim slowly along tropical rivers, estuaries, and coasts, browsing peacefully on underwater grasses and weeds.

Heavy bones help manatees to stay down in the water when they are feeding, but they come to the surface to breathe. This young manatee, nuzzling for milk between its mother's front flippers, has found out how to control its breathing. It can swim along the bottom to browse, or float up to the surface when it needs air.

This baby's main problem now is keeping clear of boats. It lives in a busy corner of the Caribbean Sea, which is used by hundreds of small pleasure craft, especially on weekends. It can easily dodge big ships or slow-moving sail boats. Real danger comes from the whizzing propellers of powerboats, which can cut and even kill a small manatee.

Newborn baby manatees are too heavy to float, and have to be helped to the surface to take their first breath.

Along crowded waterways and coasts packed with small craft, manatees often bear the scars of propellers.

Pygmy hippopotamus

Big hippopotamuses of Central and East Africa stand almost 5 feet (1.5 m) at the shoulder and can weigh almost 9,000 pounds (4 tonnes). Pygmy hippos, a much smaller species of tropical West Africa, stand only 30 inches (80 cm) at the shoulder and weigh about 500 pounds (230 kg). This baby pygmy hippo, born a few days ago and tiny as they come, could rub noses with a small pig. With its mother close by, it is just starting to find its way about the swamp that is its home.

Big hippos live in herds, but pygmy hippos tend to live on their own. This mother and baby smell and hear others of their kind, including the baby's father. But they keep their distance and seldom see strangers. They wander through the dense, damp forests, never far from water, feeding on grasses, leaves, and shoots. From time to time, they wallow along the muddy riverbanks, and swim across to new feeding areas that the mother remembers from times past.

Not many other mammals share this wet, soggy environment, but young pygmy hippos are constantly in danger from crocodiles, big snakes, and a few other predators. Even people like their meat. In a world full of larger, hungry animals, keeping to themselves is by far the safest way for pygmy hippos to live.

Standing less than 3 ft. (1 m) high, pygmy hippos are dwarfed by the tall trees of the West African rainforest.

Pushed into the water for the first time, the baby is supported by its mother.

Norway lemming

Lemmings are small rodents, like chubby, short-tailed rats. There are a dozen species, living in northern North America, Greenland, Europe, and Siberia, in the Arctic and in cold mountain regions farther south. These Norway lemmings live in Scandinavia and northwest Russia. You find them rustling in low-growing grasses and shrubs of the tundra, where they feed on shoots, leaves, and berries. In summer, they live in the open, making tracks and runways among the vegetation. In winter, they live under the snow, in burrows and chambers that protect them from the bitter cold of the outside world. There they can continue feeding and breeding. Young lemmings grow quickly, and start breeding when only a few months old. Breeding year-round, lemmings sometimes build up huge populations, which swarm across the tundra in all directions looking for food.

Throughout the summer, they are hunted by owls and skuas that swoop on them from above. In winter, the snow hides them from aerial predators. But foxes and other ground-dwelling hunters can still sniff them out and dig through the snow to find them. Here, an Arctic fox has smelled a lemming family, and is digging hard. Will it catch them? The fox will have to be quick, because the lemmings can dodge swiftly along their tunnels, and may well get away.

Fast breeding sometimes results in swarms of young lemmings trailing each other across the tundra in search of food.

Lemmings swim well when they have to, but quickly lose heat and die if they stay too long in cold water.

Orangutan

In the tropical rain forests of northern Sumatra and Borneo live these gentle apes called orangutans. They got their name, meaning old man, because a big male, standing almost 5 feet (1.5 m) tall on the ground, looks rather like a wizened, bent old man. Every year their numbers decrease, mainly because the forests in which they live are being cut for timber.

This female, with her three-month-old baby, lives in a quiet corner of the forest where the trees are still standing. She and the dozen or more orangutans that make up her group know nothing of the dangers surrounding them. Their forest is a protected reserve, so they are safe for the moment. But just a few miles away, on the other side of the river, the trees have been felled and dragged away, and the orangutans that lived there have disappeared.

Where did they go? Some of the mothers were shot, so their babies could be sold as pets. Others just disappeared.

Baby orangs sold as pets become bored and aggressive when they are older, and often have to be caged or destroyed. It is not a bright future for this mother and baby.

Above: As they grow older, male orangutans from Borneo develop large cheek flanges that broaden their faces.

Left: Pet orangs become aggressive as adults and often finish up in cages.

Impala

Try standing up and jumping more than your own height into the air. That is a trick every young impala has to learn very soon after it is born. If it fails, it is likely to be caught by a hungry lion or leopard.

Impalas are a kind of small antelope. They are related to gazelles and stand about 39 inches (1 m) tall at the shoulders. Brown above and white underneath, they have long, slender legs with powerful, springy muscles. Their large ears twist back and forth to catch sounds from any direction. Males grow graceful, spiral horns, which get a little longer and thicker each year.

Impalas feed in small herds on the plains of eastern Africa, eating grass and shoots. All the females within a herd produce their calves at about the same time, usually during the rainy season when there is plenty of grass. Calves can run with the herd within a few hours of birth, and grow quickly. If a lion attacks, the adults try to escape by leaping rather than running. Sometimes they jump straight up, sometimes forward or to one side, even twisting in midair. So it is important, very early in life, for calves to be able to leap in this way, too. A dozen antelopes leaping like mad jackrabbits is enough to confuse any predator.

A newborn impala, too weak to run or jump, lies quietly in the grass while a hungry lion searches for food.

Within a few hours, the calf is on its feet and feeding, ready to run and jump with the herd.

Rocky Mountain goat

Surefooted, and lacking any fear of heights, mountain goats take their kids wherever there is grass to be eaten.

High among the highest of the Rocky Mountains, in some of North America's coldest and windiest corners, lives a tough, long-haired species of mountain goat. As big as a large sheep and weighing 300 pounds (140 kg) or more, they live in small flocks of up to a dozen, browsing and grazing on the thin vegetation. In winter, they live close to the timberline, the upper margin of the forest. In summer, they spread over the areas of tundra, with its low shrubs and plants, and among the crags, climbing high in search of food.

Mountaineers who have labored to climb an almost vertical peak, wearing nailed climbing boots and using ice axes, ropes, and other aids, are often surprised to reach the top and find a mountain goat or two waiting for them. Broad black hooves, tough and sharp-edged, combined with lack of fear and an extraordinary sense of balance, get these animals into the most extreme places, young and old alike.

Mountain goats learn early. This kid, just a few days old, is already practicing its leaps. In a few days' time, it will be following its mother along narrow tracks, racing up and down the loose scree slopes, and leaping fearlessly from rock to rock like an experienced adult goat. Don't try it – it might look easy, but it's a dangerous way to live.

Sharp-edged hooves and a sense of balance help this kid to teeter on a loose boulder without falling.

Giant panda

The temperate bamboo forests of southern China, warm in summer but cold in winter, are the home of these furry black-and-white animals. Related to bears, and bearlike in many ways, giant pandas are mainly vegetarian. They live almost entirely on young bamboo shoots, grasses, and other nourishing vegetation. Winter and summer alike, they munch constantly during the daylight hours. Each panda needs a large area of forest to feed in, and the right kind of bamboo shoots to munch.

A thick furry coat protects giant pandas from the coldest winter weather. They watch the world through tiny brown eyes, ringed with a broad circle of black or dark brown fur. Once plentiful, these unusual animals are now rather scarce. Not many pandas remain in their old haunts. Though popular in zoos, mainly for their appealing faces, they are dull, sleepy animals, seldom exerting themselves except to pull down another bamboo stem.

Baby pandas, tiny at birth, are pink and almost naked for the first few weeks of life. They grow quickly to a comfortable, cuddly stage, in which an attentive mother carries and nurses them fondly. Soon they learn to feed over her shoulder, acquiring a taste for the bamboo that will become their main diet throughout life. Though protected by law, they are still hunted, because it is difficult to police the remote forest areas where they live.

Panda cubs are almost naked for the first few weeks of life.

During their first few years, young pandas climb trees when alarmed. Later they grow too heavy.

Triops

Triops, meaning three-eyed, is the name given to a small crustacean about 1 inch (2.5 cm) long that lives in shallow pools in temperate and tropical regions. Related to shrimp and crabs, it looks vaguely like the trilobites that we know only as fossils. It may well be a modern descendant of those ancient creatures.

These triops live in a pool in the Mojave Desert of southern California. Greeny-gray, with dozens of legs under that transparent shell, there is nothing special about their appearance. Their most remarkable quality is an ability to withstand drying out. Pools seldom last long in deserts. They form on the rare occasions when it rains, and dry out within hours or days. Then they reappear during the next spell of rain, which in a desert may come next month, next year, or fifty years later.

Animals that live in desert pools must be able to survive these long dry spells. Triops's secret is to lay tough-shelled eggs as the pond dries. Although the living animals die and fall to dust, the eggs survive year after year in the dry pond mud. Then they hatch with the next rain, producing young that are themselves mature and ready to lay eggs within two to three weeks. In this process millions die, but millions more are left to carry on.

Tiny triops eggs live for many years in the dried-out mud of temporary desert ponds.

Maned wolf

This rare, elegant animal lives in the grasslands of southern Brazil and Argentina. More like a fox than a wolf – perhaps a fox in high heels – it stands 30 inches (75 cm) tall, with a long nose, long ears, and a long bushy tail. The "mane" is little more than a dense furry collar on a thin, tawny-brown coat.

We know very little about the maned wolf's way of life. You seldom see them during the day. Like most other foxes, they emerge during the evening, and spend the night hunting small mammals and reptiles in the long grass. Rather surprisingly, they also eat fruit. In zoos, they especially enjoy bananas. Vixens produce litters of two or three puppies, which have short, normal legs for their size. Those long shanks come with adolescence. Maned wolves can run fast, but sadly not fast enough to avoid almost certain extinction in the wild before very long.

The trouble? They are said to kill lambs, chickens, and other domestic stock, which is probably true. In return, the farmers and stockmen run them down on horseback, shoot them as vermin, and kill them in their dens. Local conservationists in South America would like to help them, but they have no money, and the rest of the world has other things to worry about. Maned wolves are just one more attractive, interesting species that will almost certainly disappear from the wild.

Maned wolf puppies have relatively short legs, which grow longer toward the end of their first year, when they reach maturity.

Index